2ND EDITION

FOR ORGANS, PIANOS & ELECTRONIC KEYBOARDS

E·Z PLAY TODAY
37

FAVORITE
LATIN SONGS
(CANCIONES FAVORITAS)

ISBN-13: 978-0-7935-2564-5
ISBN-10: 0-7935-2564-0

HAL•LEONARD®
CORPORATION
7777 W. BLUEMOUND RD. P.O. BOX 13819 MILWAUKEE, WI 53213

Visit Hal Leonard Online at
www.halleonard.com

Água De Beber
(Water to Drink)

Registration 8
Rhythm: Bossa Nova or Latin

English Words by Norman Gimbel
Portuguese Words by Vinicius de Moraes
Music by Antonio Carlos Jobim

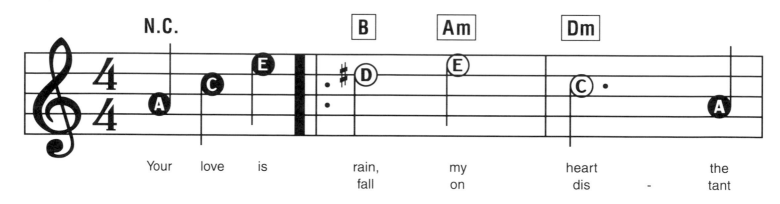

Your love is rain, my heart the
fall on dis - tant

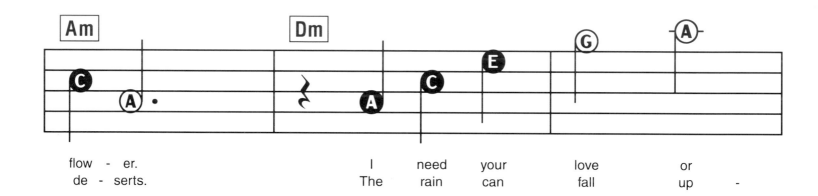

flow - er. I need your love or
de - serts. The rain can fall up -

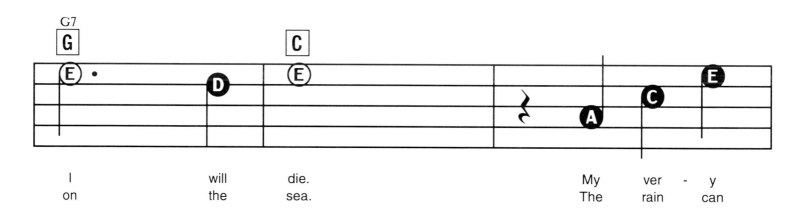

I will die. My ver - y
on the sea. The rain can

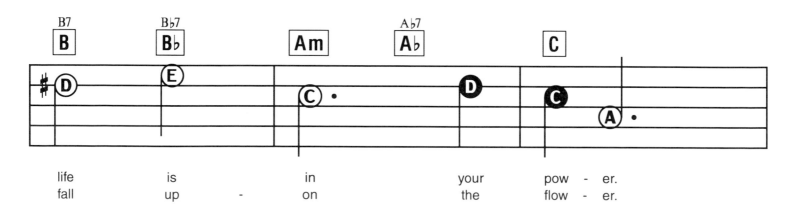

life is in your pow - er.
fall up - on the flow - er.

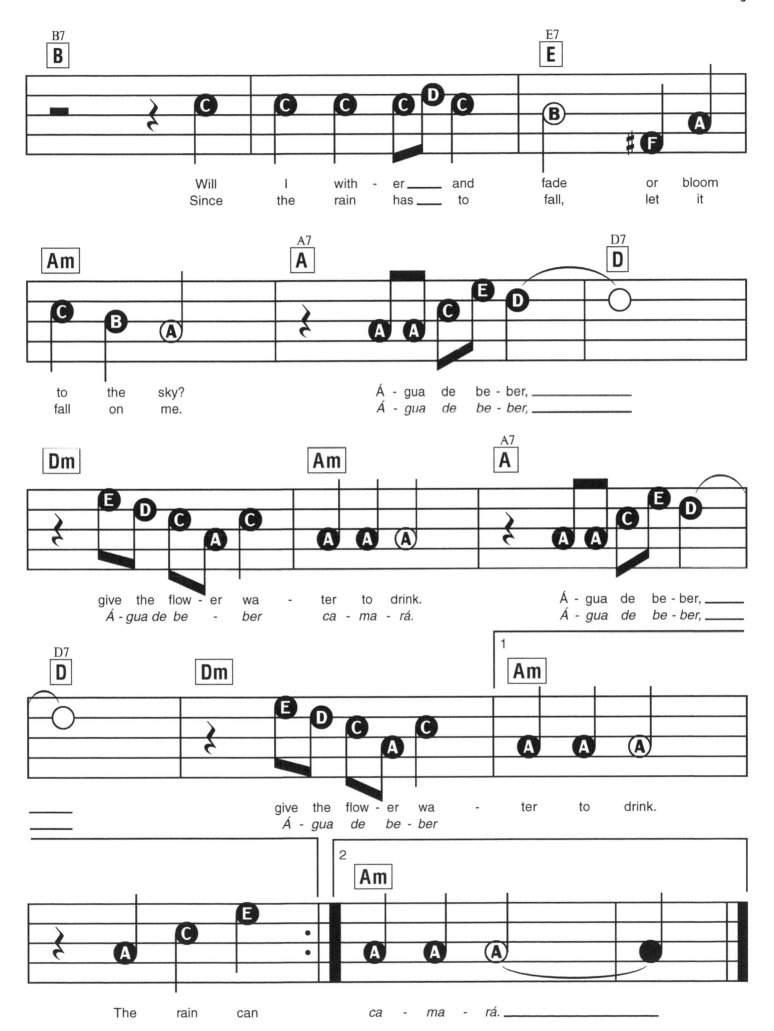

Amapola
(Pretty Little Poppy)

Registration 3
Rhythm: Latin or Rhumba

By Joseph M. Lacalle
New English Words by Albert Gamse

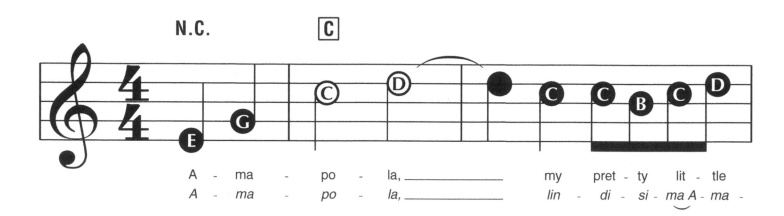

A - ma - po - la, _____ my pret-ty lit - tle
A - ma - po - la, _____ lin - di - si - ma A - ma -

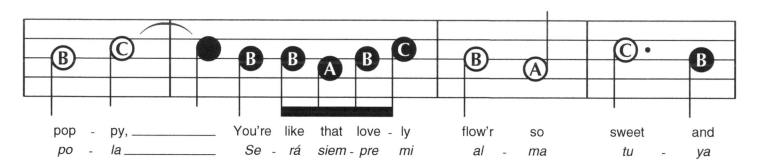

pop - py, _____ You're like that love - ly flow'r so sweet and
po - la _____ Se - rá siem-pre mi al - ma tu - ya

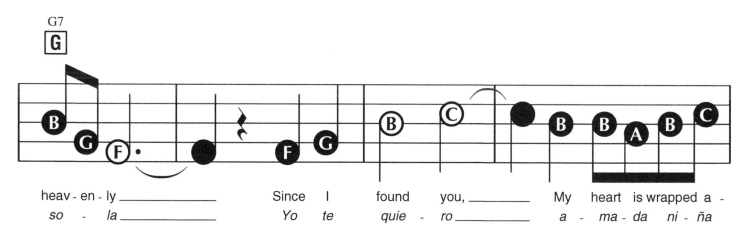

heav - en - ly _____ Since I found you, _____ My heart is wrapped a -
so - la _____ Yo te quie - ro _____ a - ma - da ni - ña

round you _____ And lov - ing you, it seems to
mi - a _____ I - gual que a - ma la flor la

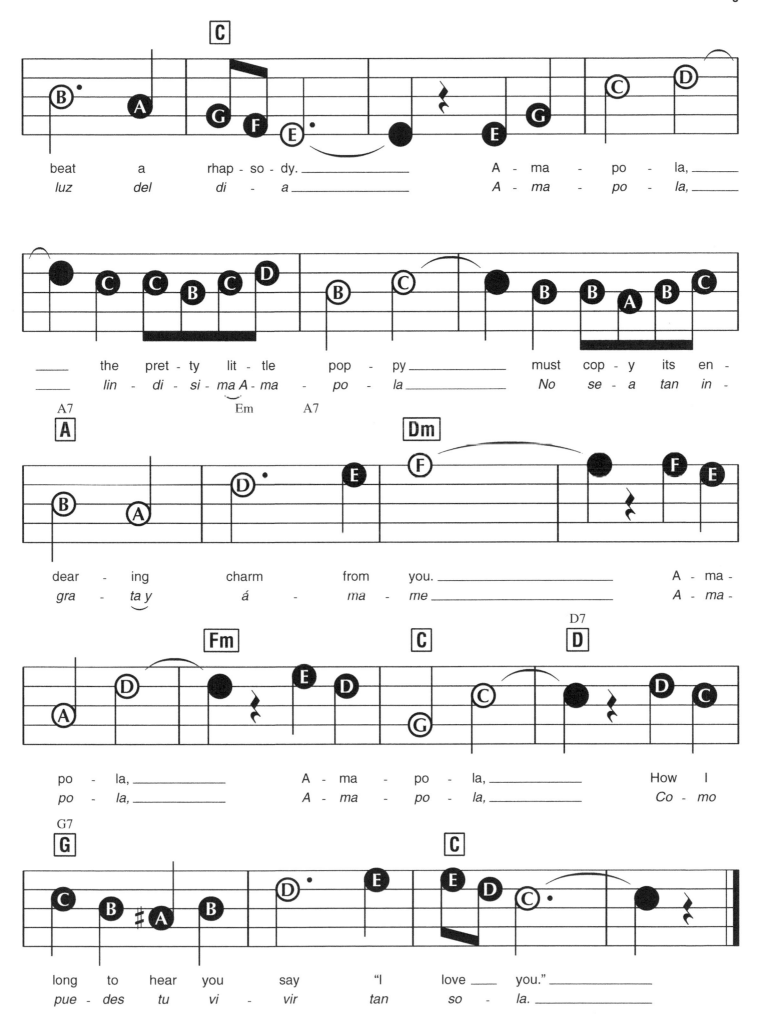

Bésame Mucho
(Kiss Me Much)

Registration 1
Rhythm: Rhumba or Latin

Music and Spanish Words by Consuelo Velazquez
English Words by Sunny Skylar

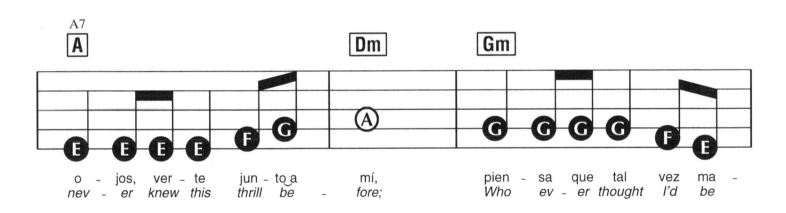

D.C. al Fine
(Return to beginning
Play to Fine)

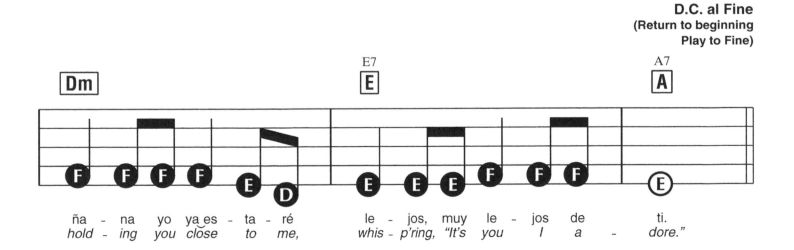

The Constant Rain
(Chove Chuva)

Registration 2
Rhythm: Samba or Latin

Original Words and Music by Jorge Ben
English Words by Norman Gimbel

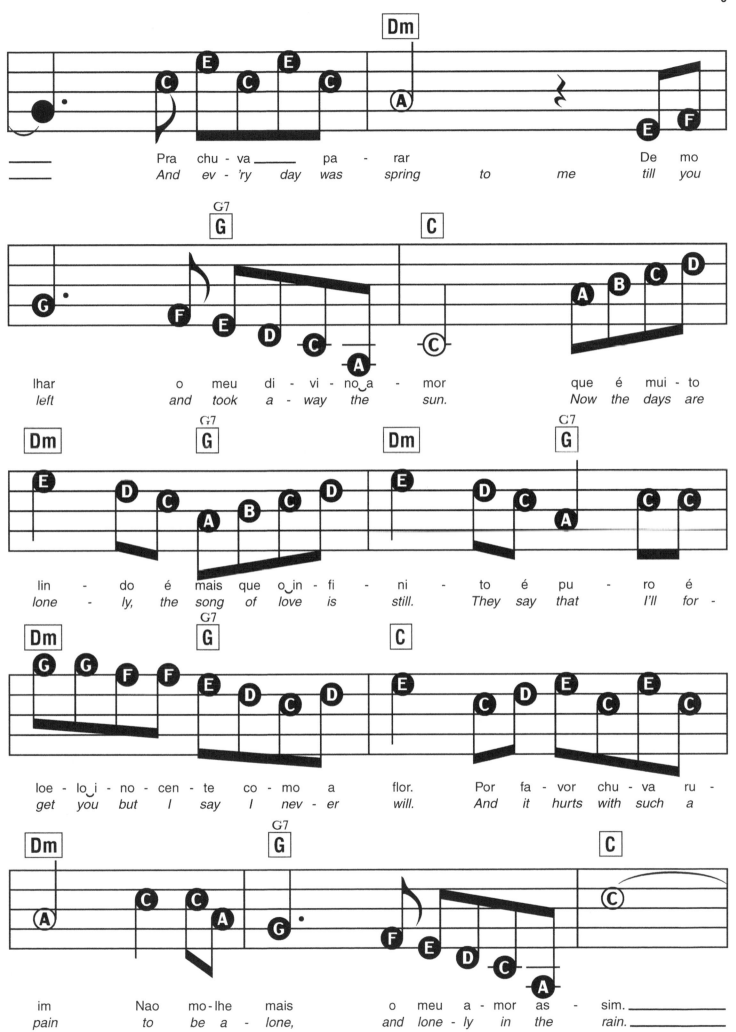

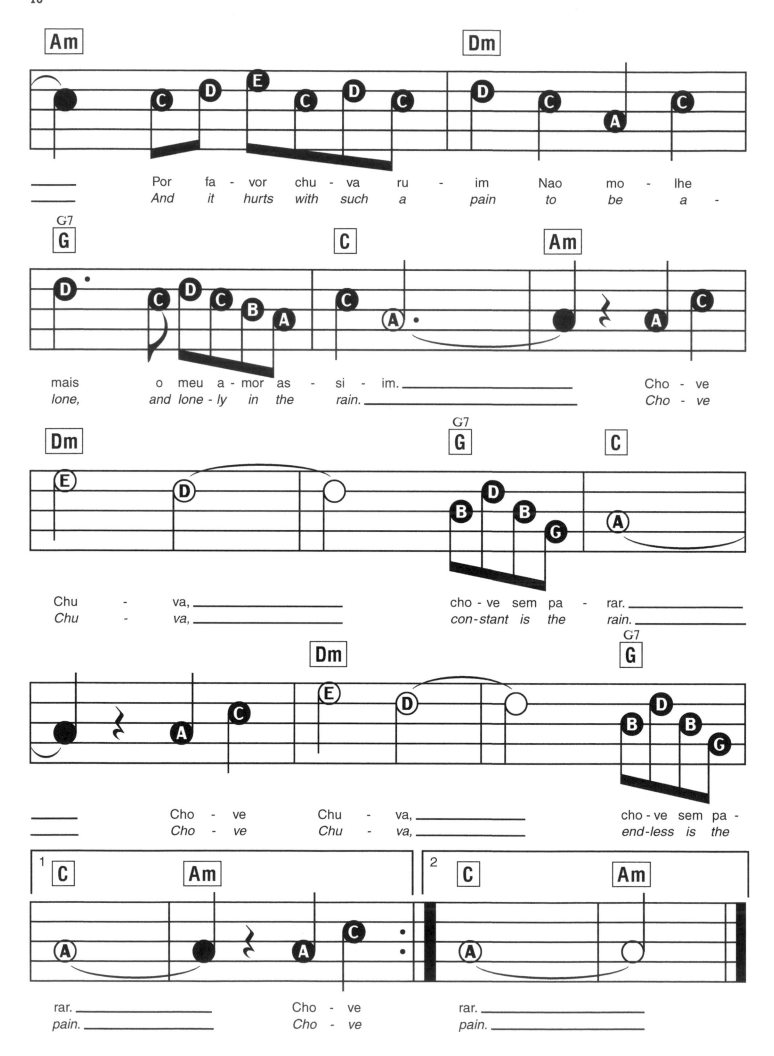

Frenesí

Registration 2
Rhythm: Rhumba or Latin

Words and Music by
Alberto Dominguez

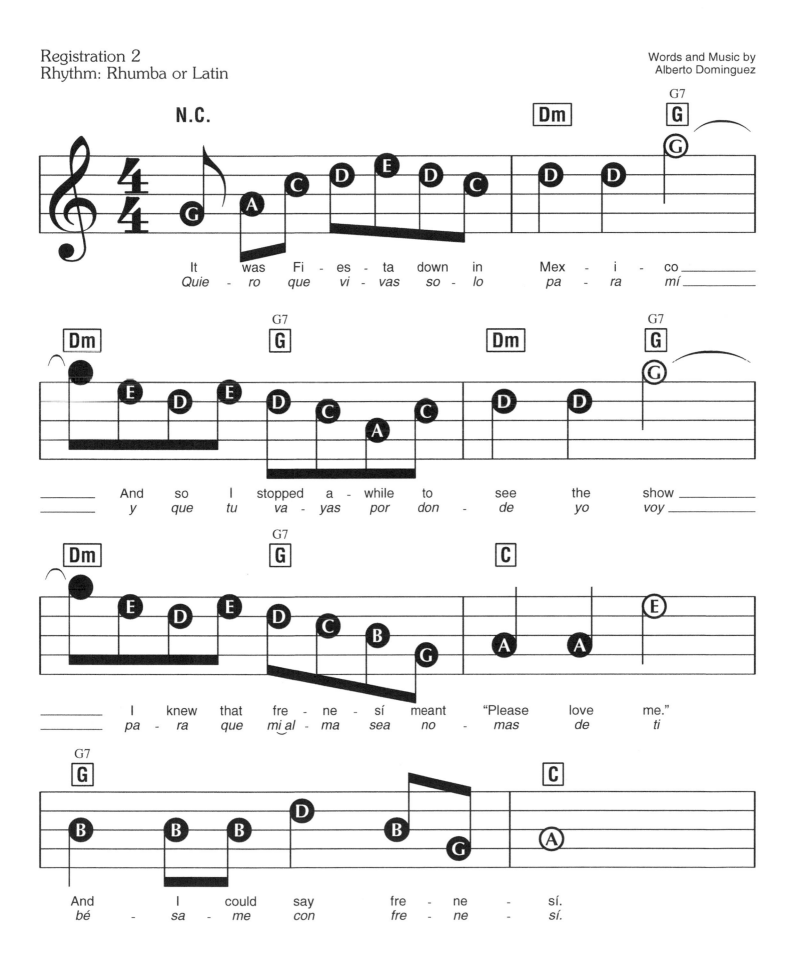

13

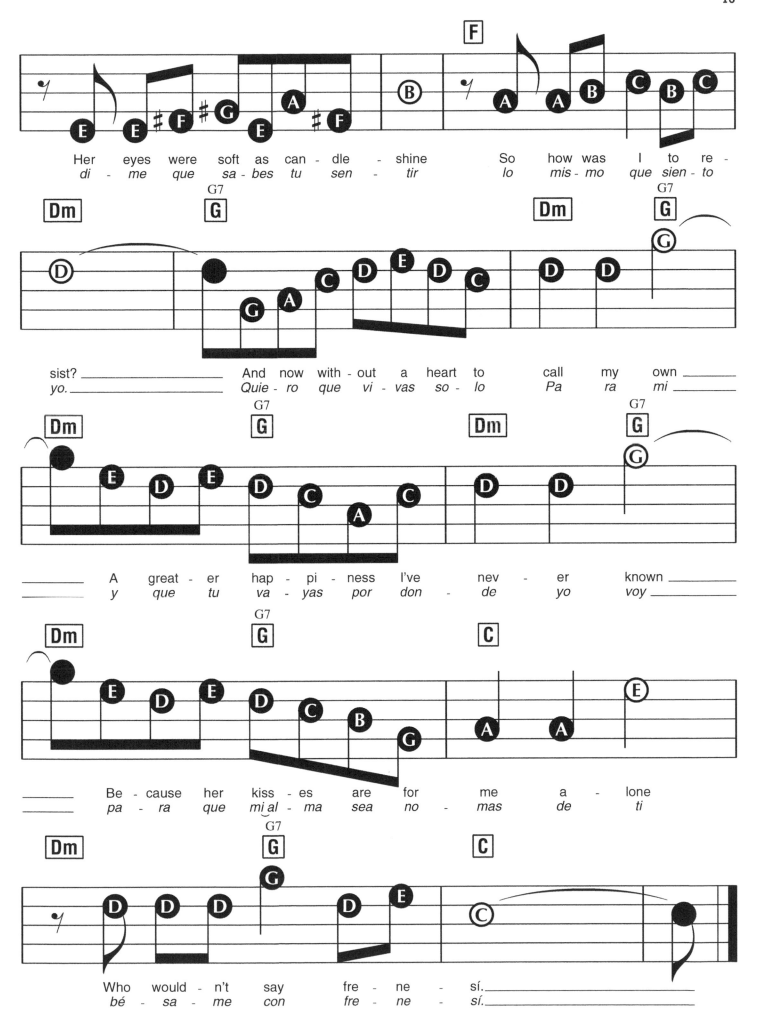

Cuando Calienta El Sol
(Love Me with All Your Heart)

Registration 9
Rhythm: Rhumba or Latin

Original Words and Music by Carlos Rigual and Carlos A. Martinoli
English Words by Sunny Skylar

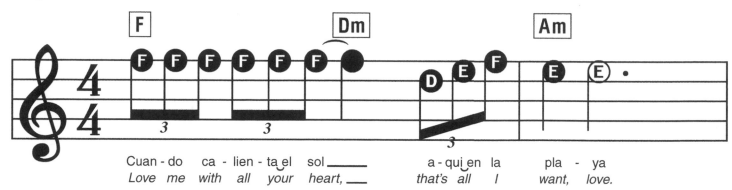

Cuan - do ca - lien - ta el sol _____ a - qui en la pla - ya
Love me with all your heart, ___ that's all I want, love.

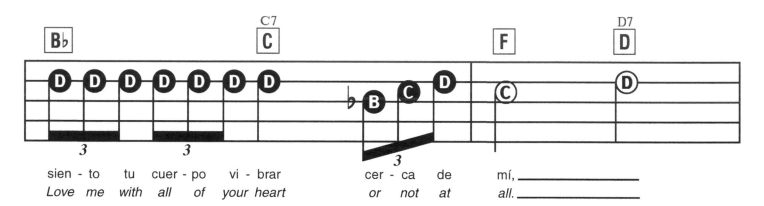

sien - to tu cuer - po vi - brar cer - ca de mí, _____
Love me with all of your heart or not at all. _____

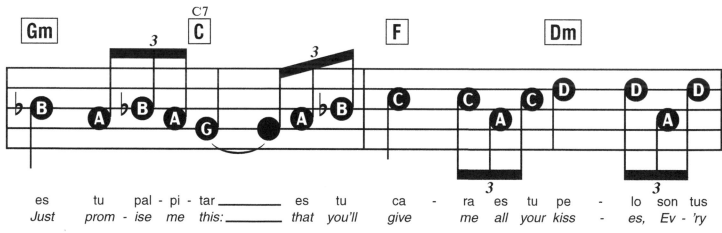

es tu pal - pi - tar _____ es tu ca - ra es tu pe - lo son tus
Just prom - ise me this: _____ that you'll give me all your kiss - es, Ev - 'ry

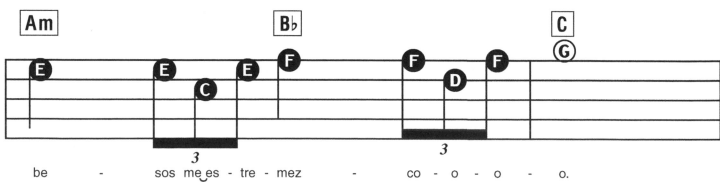

be - sos me es - tre - mez - co - o - o - o.
win - ter, ev - 'ry sum - mer, ev - 'ry fall.

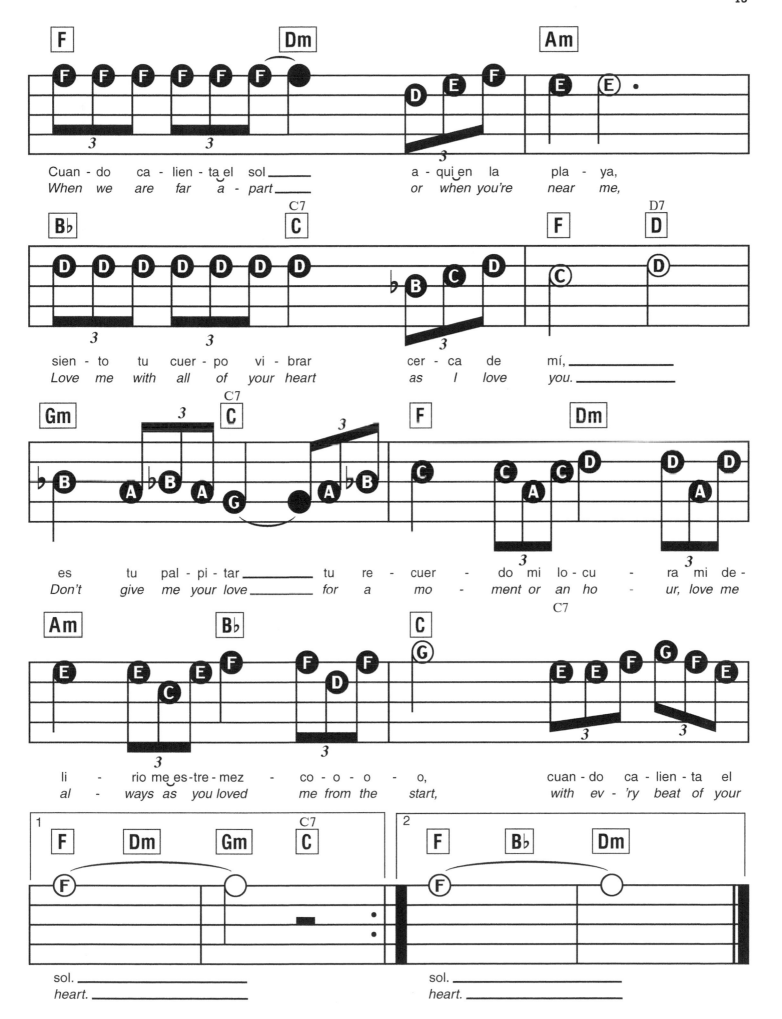

Desafinado
(Slightly Out of Tune)

Registration 8
Rhythm: Bossa Nova

English Lyric by Jon Hendricks and Jessie Cavanaugh
Original Text by Newton Mendonca
Music by Antonio Carlos Jobim

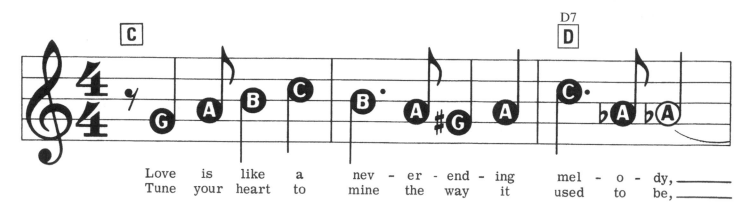

Love is like a nev-er-end-ing mel-o-dy,____
Tune your heart to mine the way it used to be,____

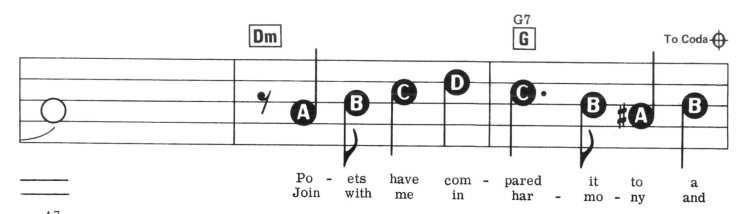

____ Po-ets have com-pared it to a
Join with me in har-mo-ny and

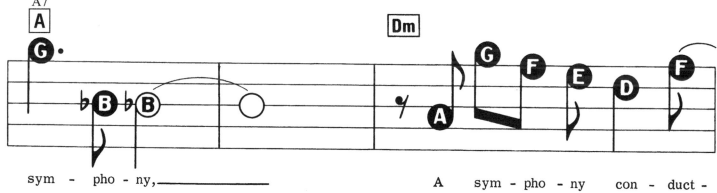

sym-pho-ny,____ A sym-pho-ny con-duct-

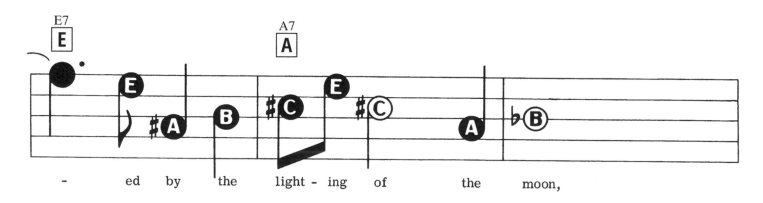

-ed by the light-ing of the moon,

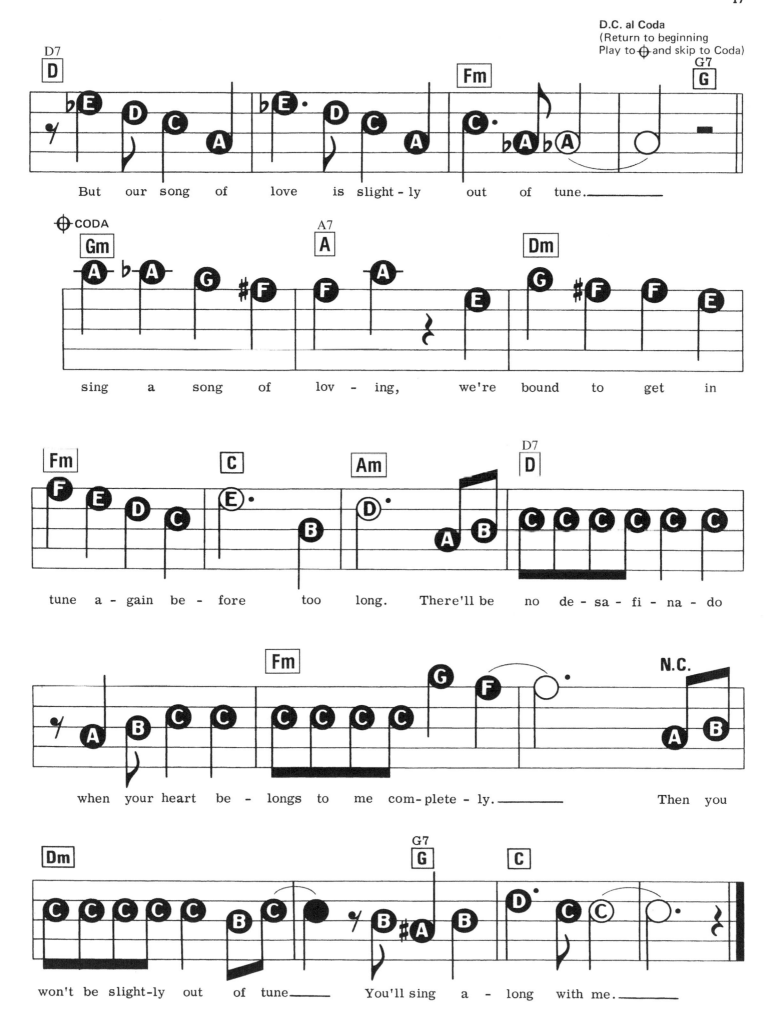

The Girl from Ipanema
(Garôta De Ipanema)

Registration 4
Rhythm: Latin or Bossa Nova

Music by Antonio Carlos Jobim
English Words by Norman Gimbel
Original Words by Vinicius de Moraes

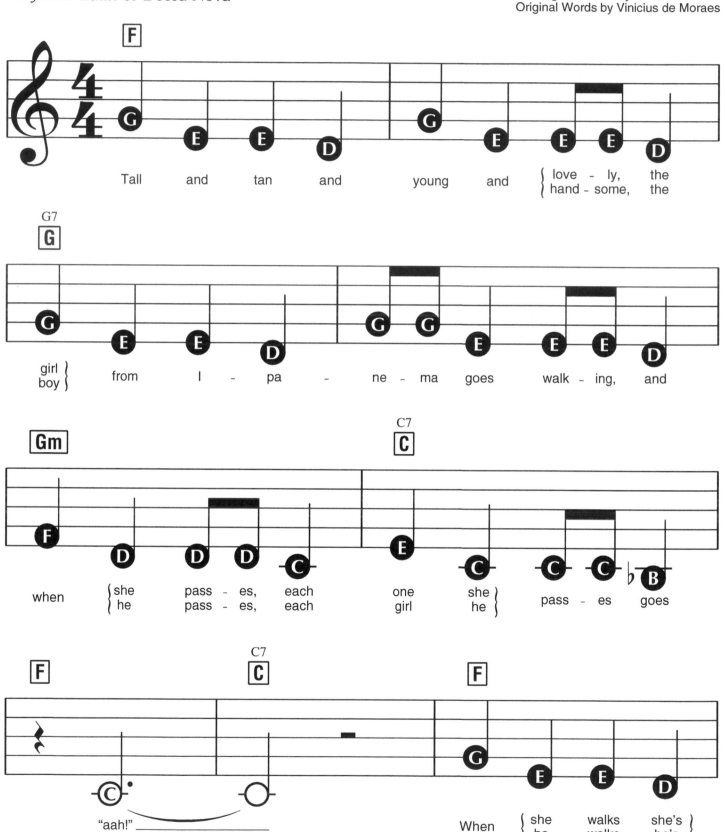

19

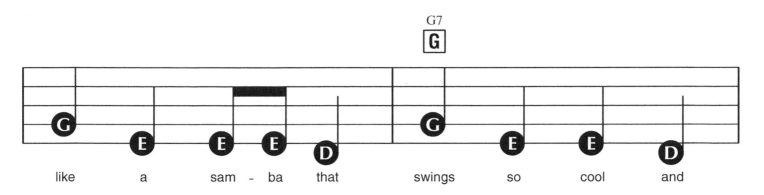

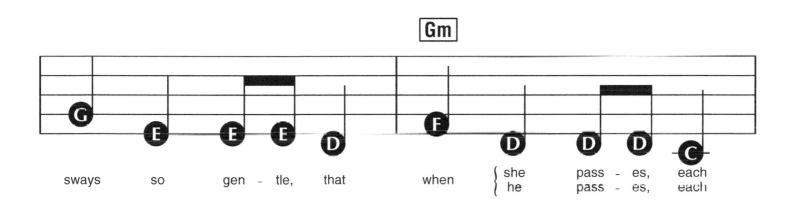

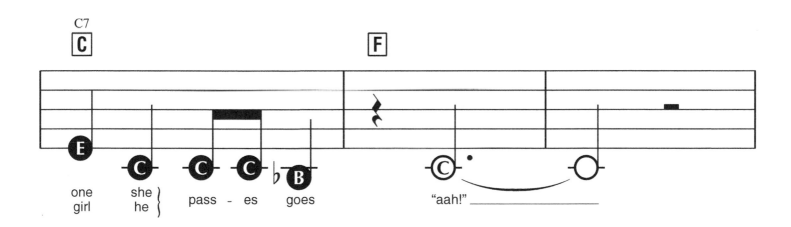

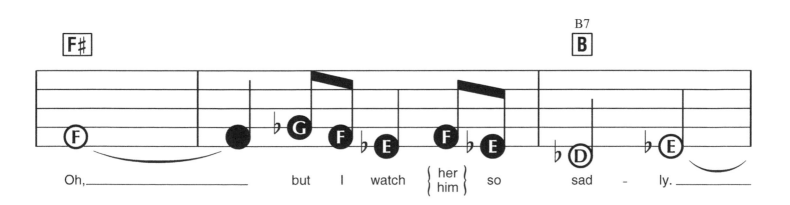

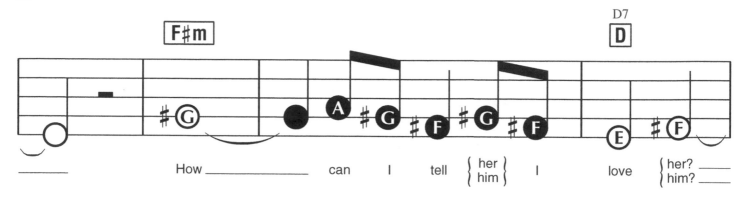

How _____ can I tell { her him } I love { her? him? } _____

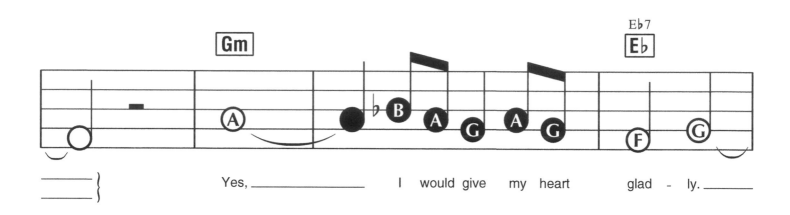

_____ } Yes, _____ I would give my heart glad - ly. _____

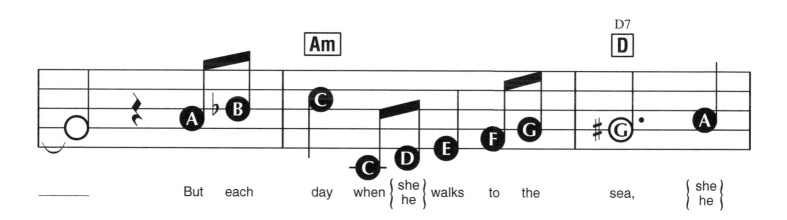

_____ But each day when { she he } walks to the sea, { she he }

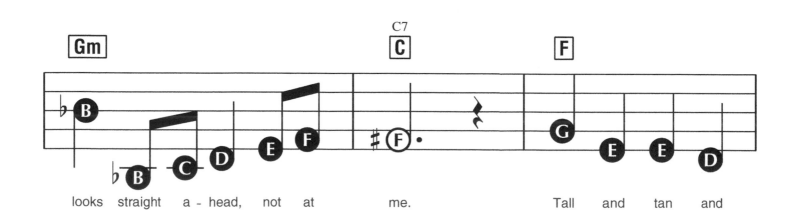

looks straight a - head, not at me. Tall and tan and

21

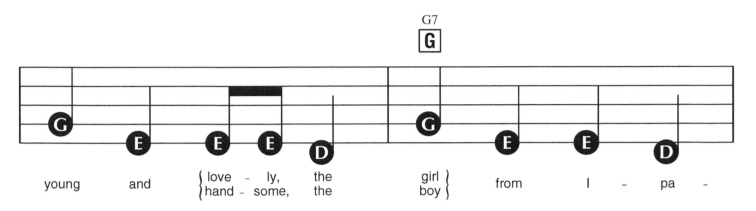

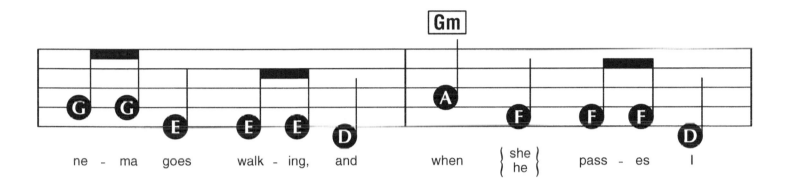

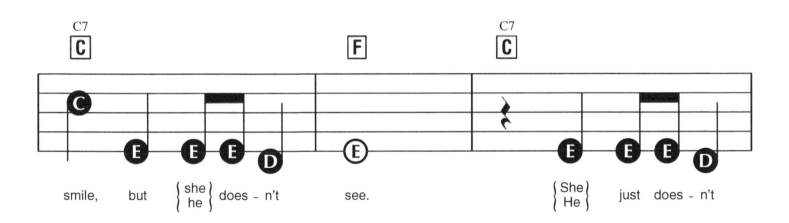

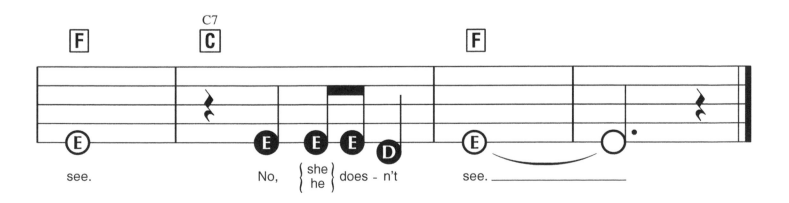

How Insensitive
(Insensatez)

Music by Antonio Carlos Jobim
Original Words by Vinicius de Moraes
English Words by Norman Gimbel

Registration 8
Rhythm: Bossa Nova or Latin

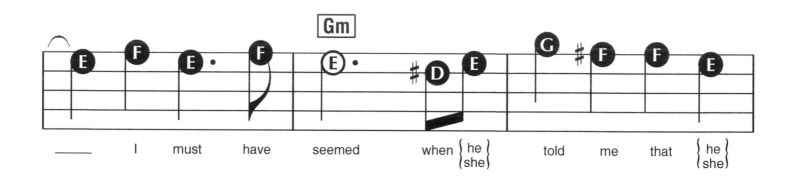

How _____ in - sen - si - tive _____

_____ I must have seemed when {he}{she} told me that {he}{she}

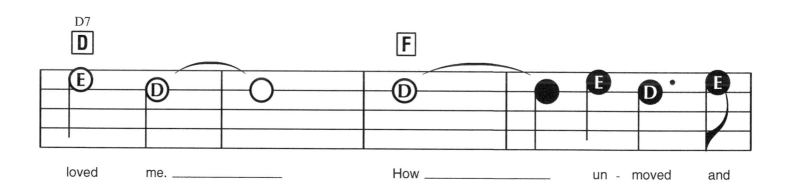

loved me. _____ How _____ un - moved and

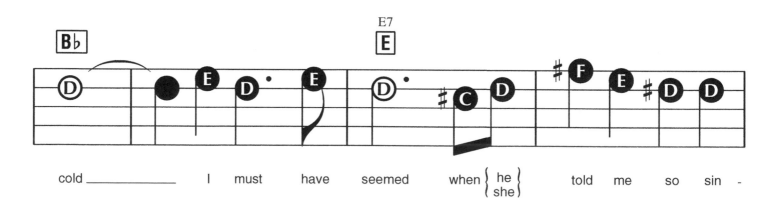

cold _____ I must have seemed when {he}{she} told me so sin -

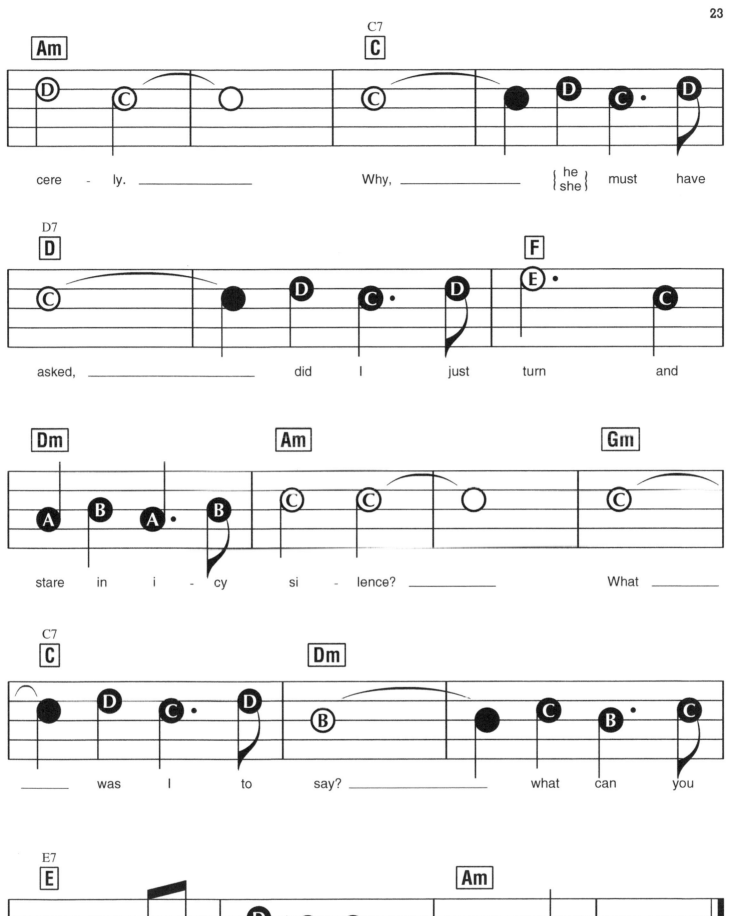

La Cumparsita
(The Masked One)

Registration 7
Rhythm: Tango

Words and Music by Gerardo Matos Rodriquez,
Pascual Contursi and Enrique Pedro Moroni

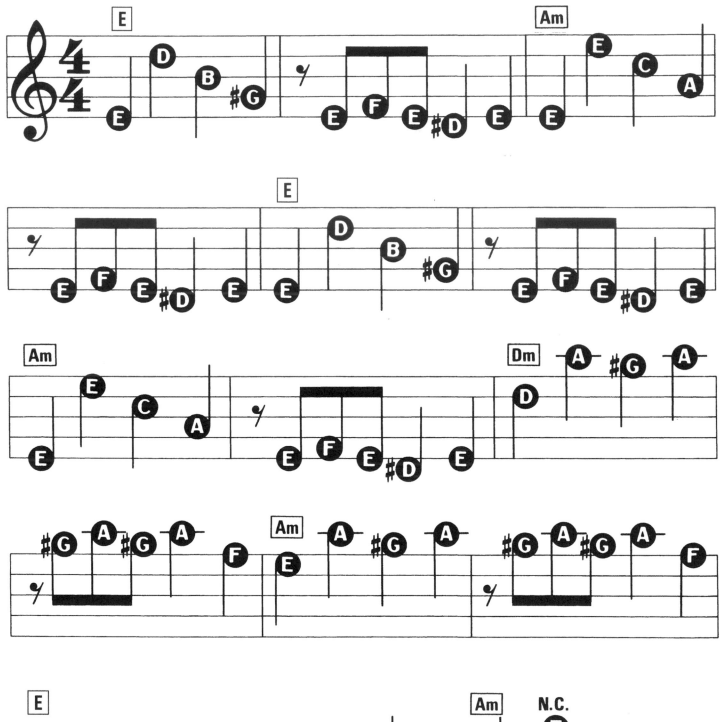

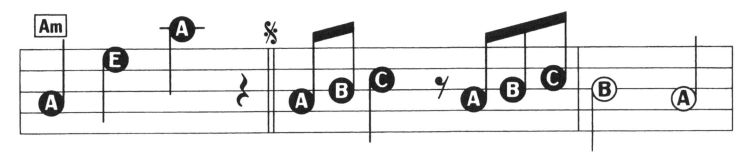

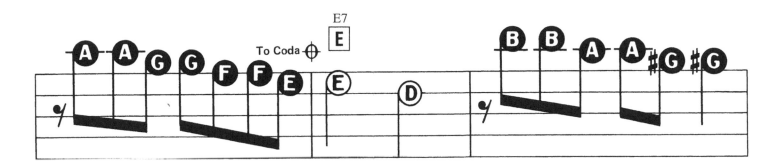

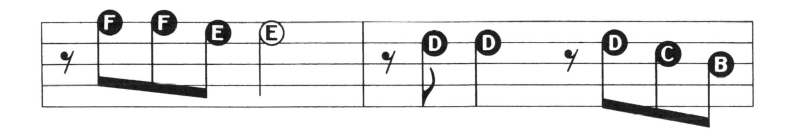

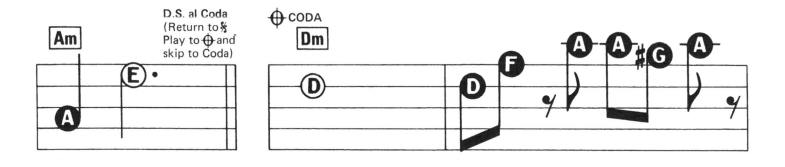

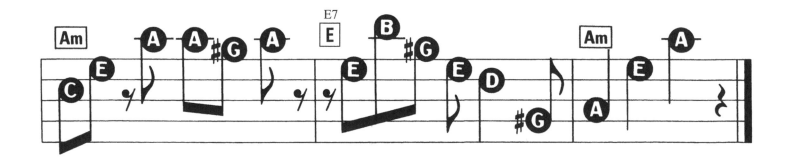

Lisbon Antigua
(In Old Lisbon)

Registration 1
Rhythm: Fox Trot

English Lyric by Harry Dupree
Music by Raul Portela, J. Galhardo and Amadeu Do Vale

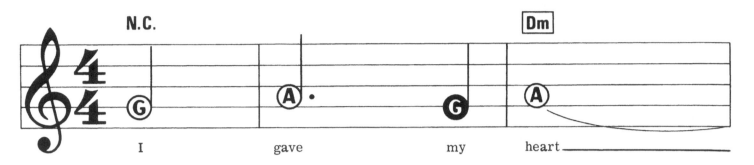

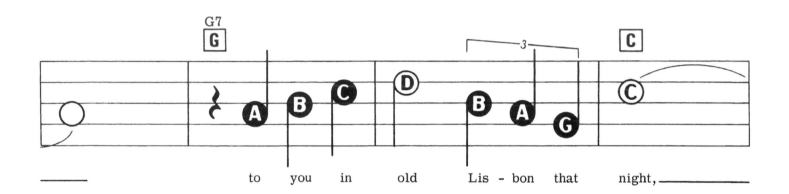

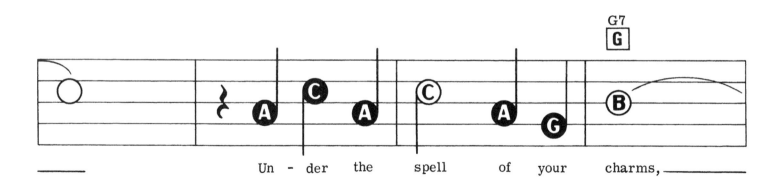

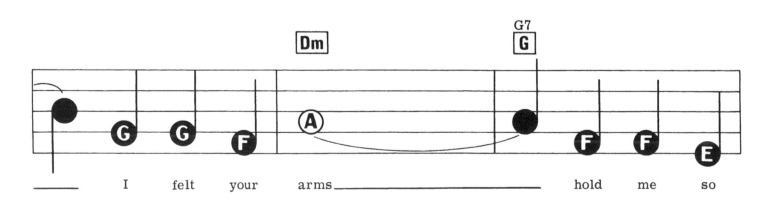

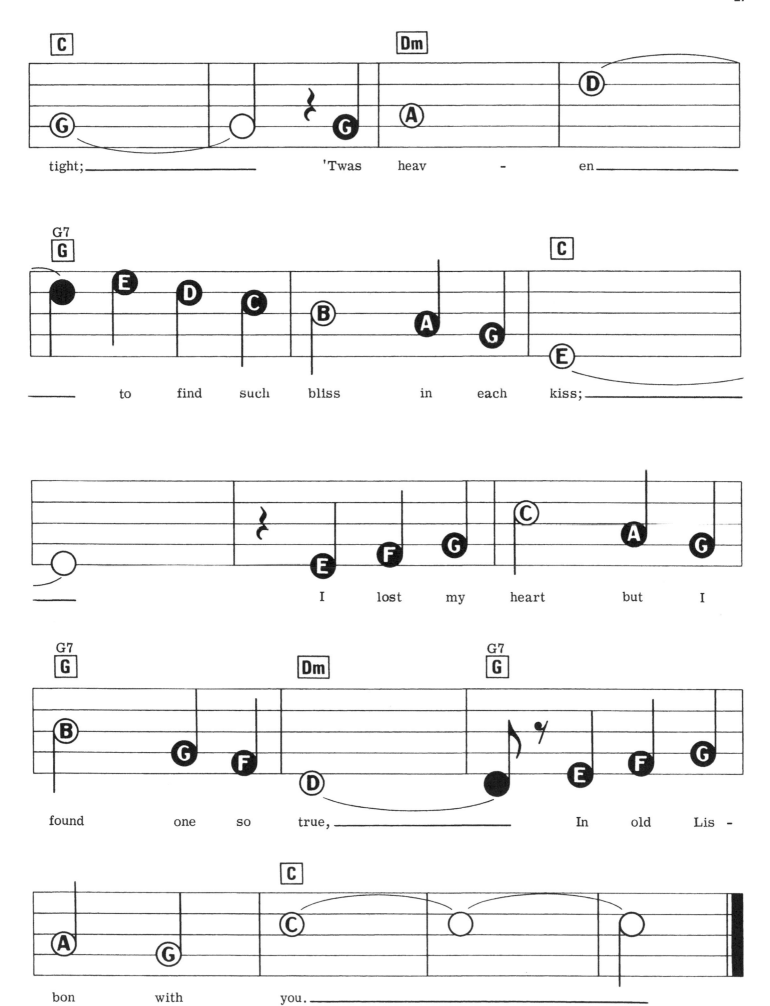

Maria Elena

Registration 10
Rhythm: Waltz

English Words by S.K. Russell
Music and Spanish Words by Lorenzo Barcelata

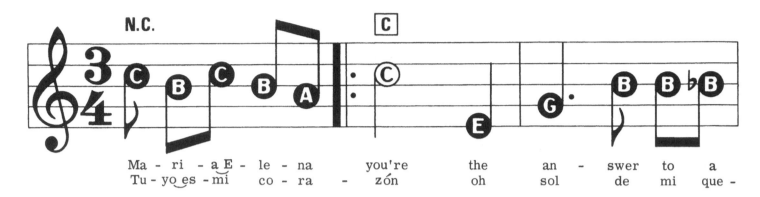

Ma - ri - a E - le - na you're the an - swer to a
Tu - yo es - mi co - ra - zón oh sol de mi que -

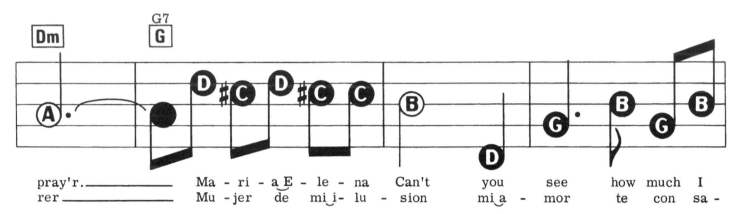

pray'r._____ Ma - ri - a E - le - na Can't you see how much I
rer_____ Mu - jer de mi i - lu - sion mi a - mor te con sa -

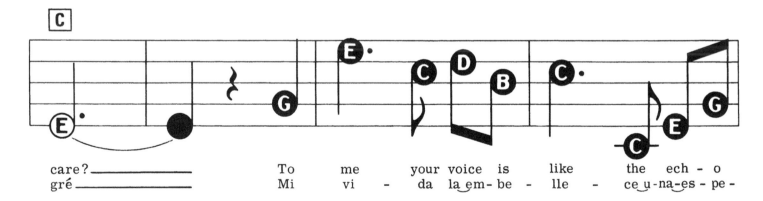

care?_____ To me your voice is like the ech - o
gré_____ Mi vi - da la em - be - lle - ce u - na es - pe -

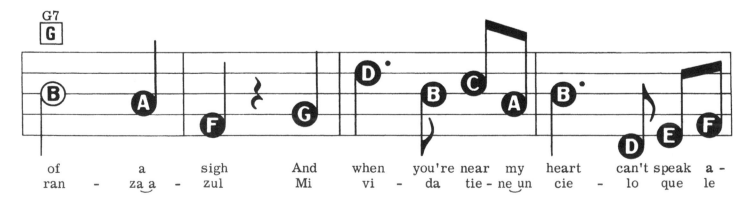

of a sigh And when you're near my heart can't speak a -
ran - za a - zul Mi vi - da tie - ne un cie - lo que le

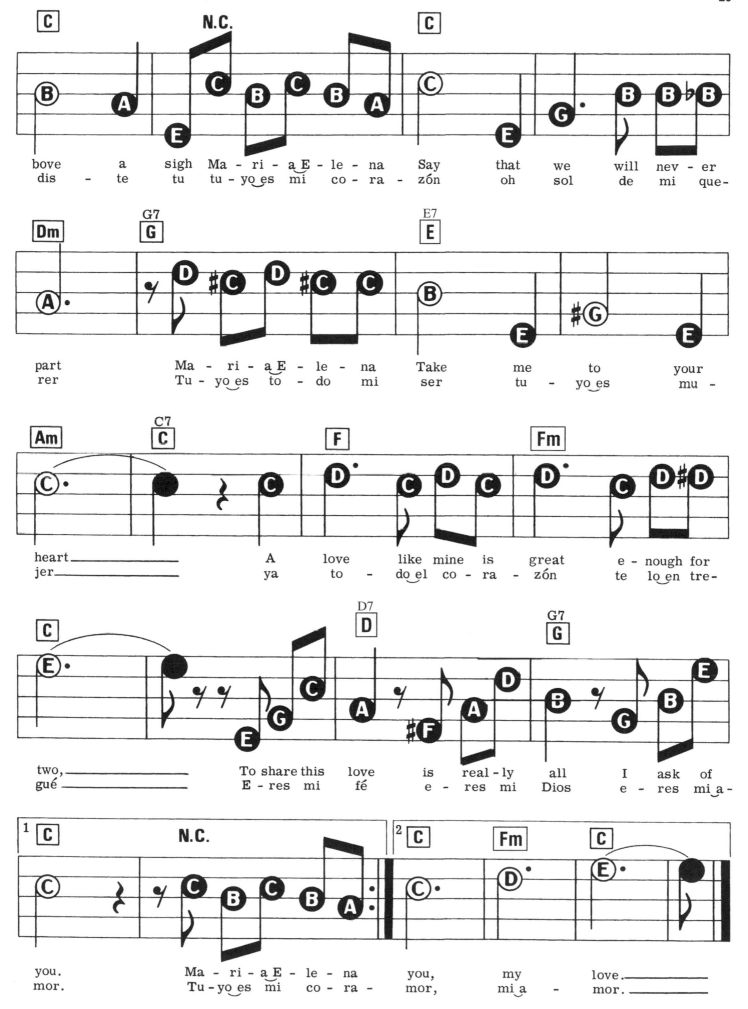

Mas Que Nada

Registration 4
Rhythm: Bossa Nova or Latin

Words and Music by
Jorge Ben

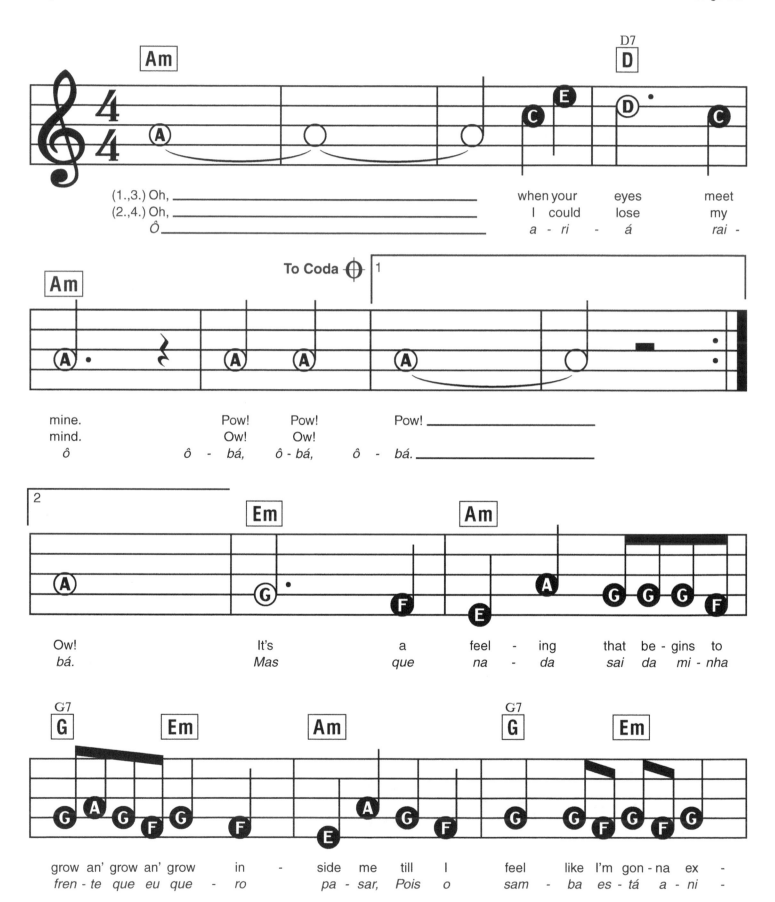

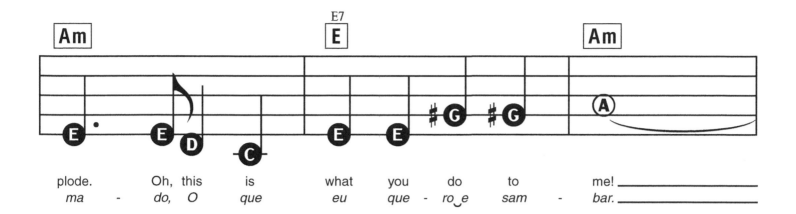

plode. Oh, this is what you do to me! _____
ma - do, O que eu que - ro͜e sam - bar. _____

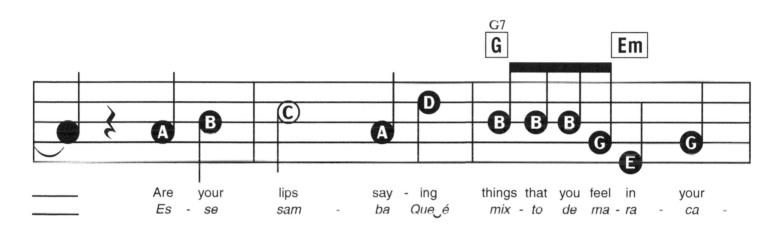

___ Are your lips say - ing things that you feel in your
___ *Es - se sam - ba Que͜é mix - to de ma - ra - ca -*

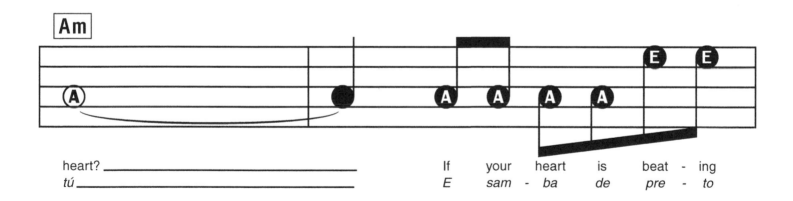

heart? _____
tú _____
          If your heart is beat - ing
          E sam - ba de pre - to

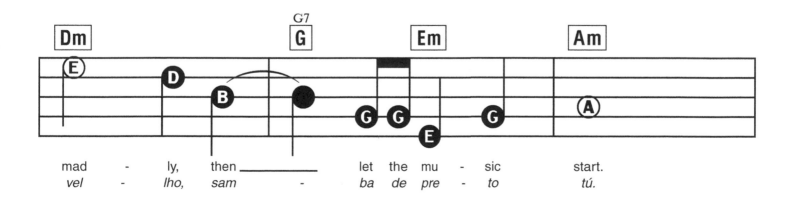

mad - ly, then _____ let the mu - sic start.
vel - lho, sam - ba de pre - to tú.

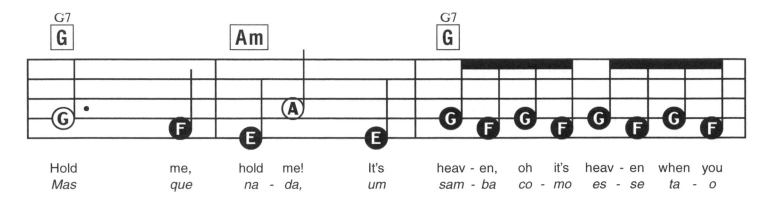

Hold me, hold me! It's heav-en, oh it's heav-en when you
Mas que na - da, um sam - ba co - mo es - se ta - o

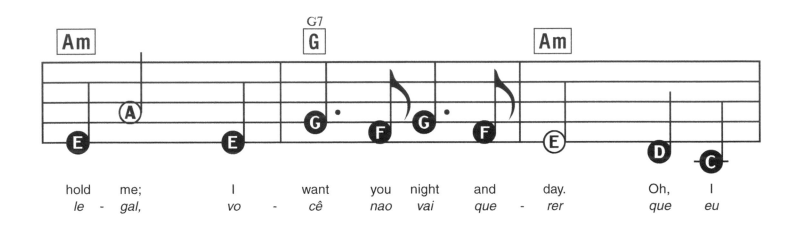

hold me; I want you night and day. Oh, I
le - gal, vo - cê nao vai que - rer que eu

D.C. al Coda
(Return to beginning
Play to ⊕ and
Skip to Coda)

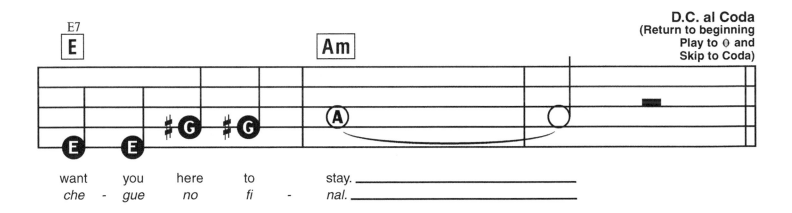

want you here to stay. _____
che - gue no fi - nal. _____

CODA

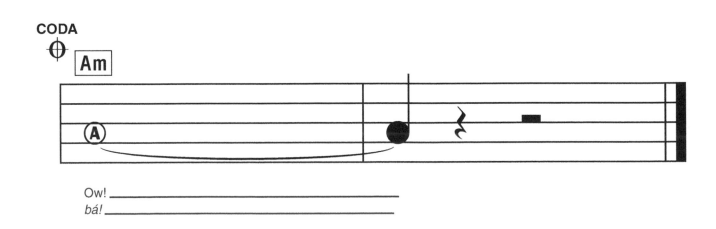

Ow! _____
bá! _____

Sway
(Quien Será)

Registration 2
Rhythm: Rhumba or Latin

English Words by Norman Gimbel
Spanish Words and Music by Pablo Beltran Ruiz

34

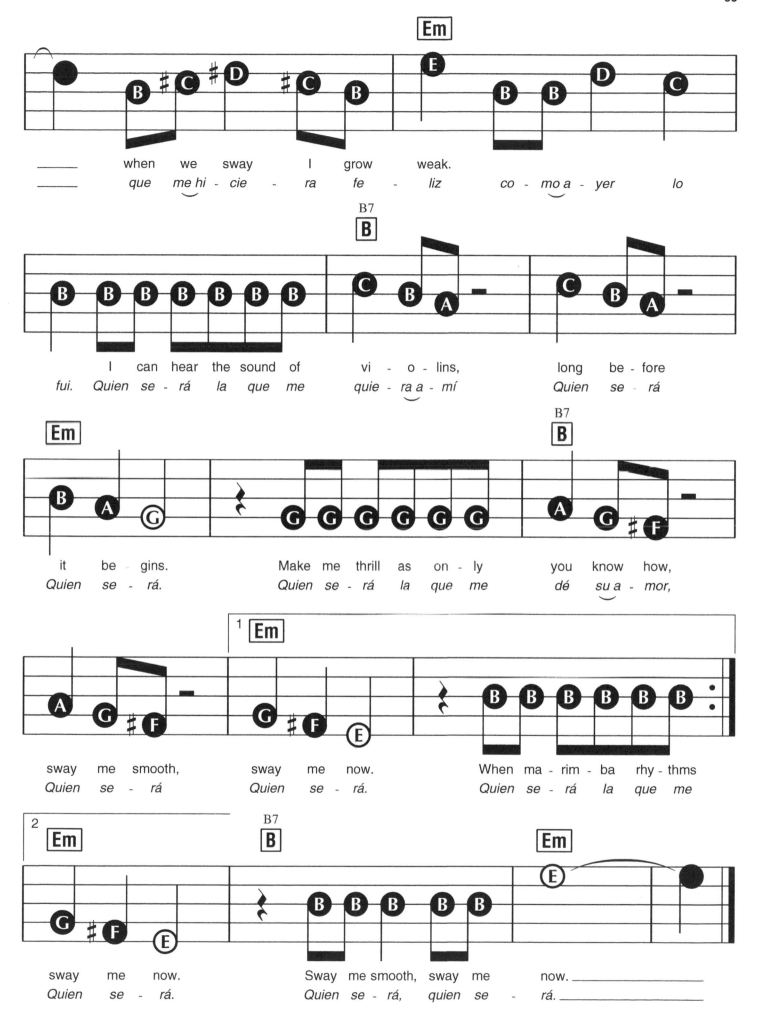

Meditation
(Meditacáo)

Registration 5
Rhythm: Rhumba or Latin

Music by Antonio Carlos Jobim
Original Words by Newton Mendonca
English Words by Norman Gimbel

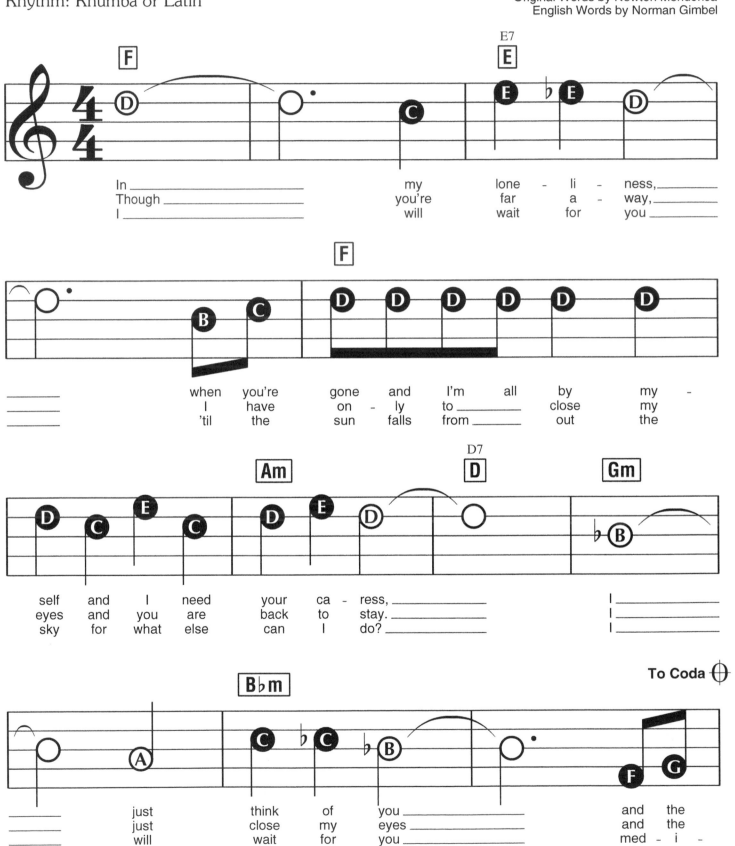

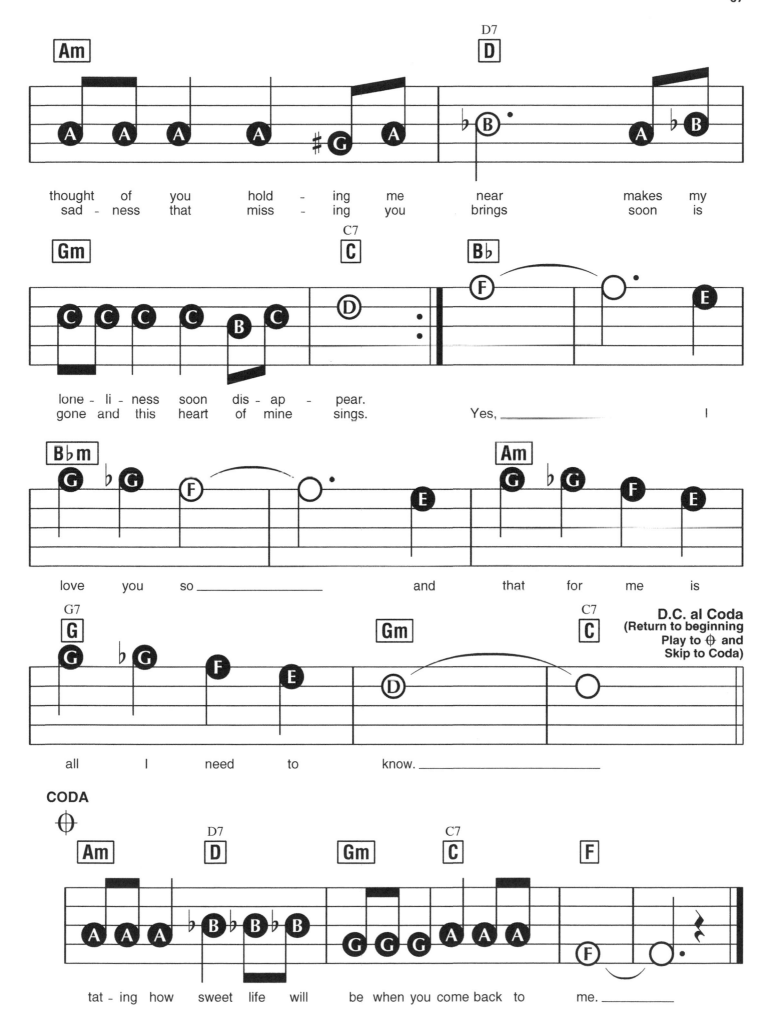

Quizás, Quizás, Quizás
(Perhaps, Perhaps, Perhaps)

Registration 4
Rhythm: Cha-Cha

Music and Spanish Words by Osvaldo Farres
English Words by Joe Davis

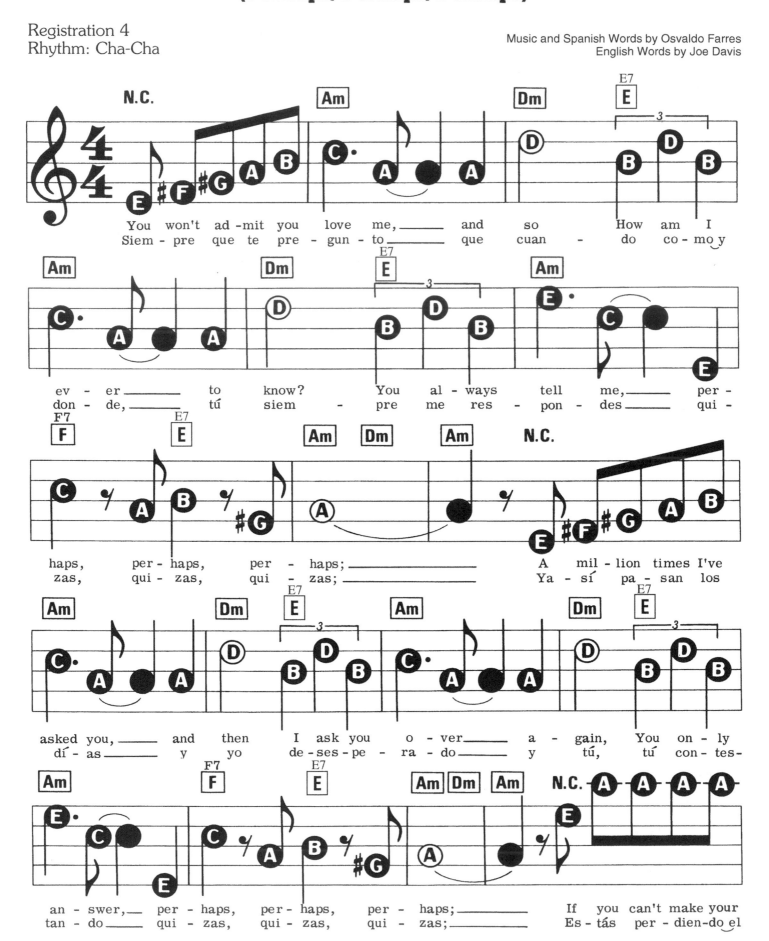

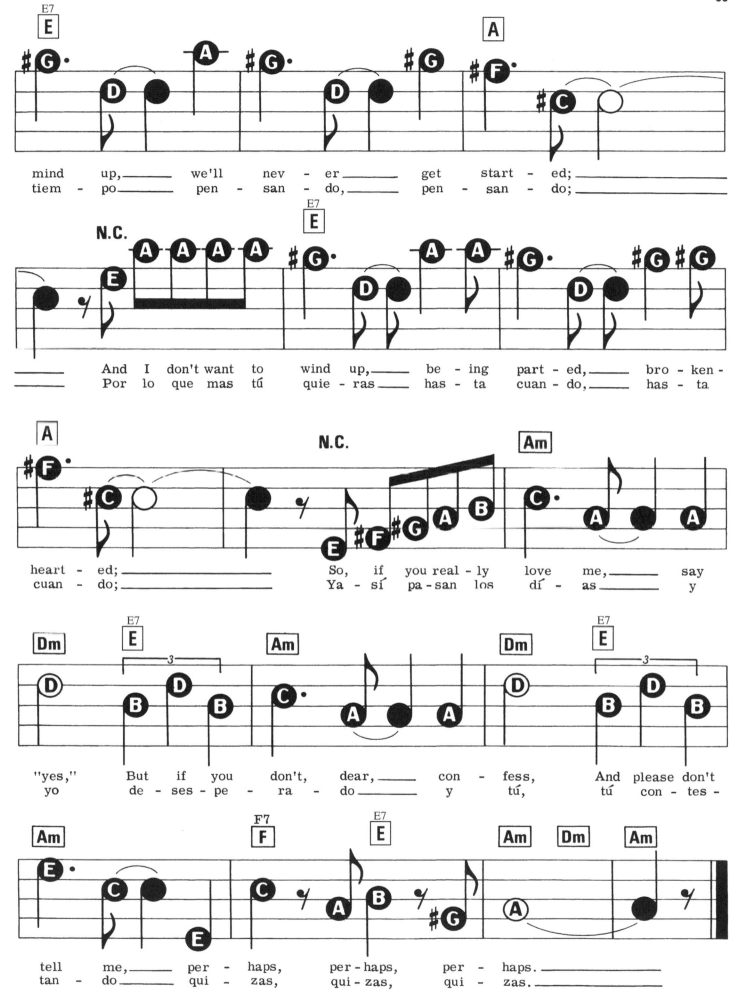

So Nice
(Summer Samba)

Registration 2
Rhythm: Bossa Nova

Original Words and Music by Marcos Valle
and Paulo Sergio Valle
English Words by Norman Gimbel

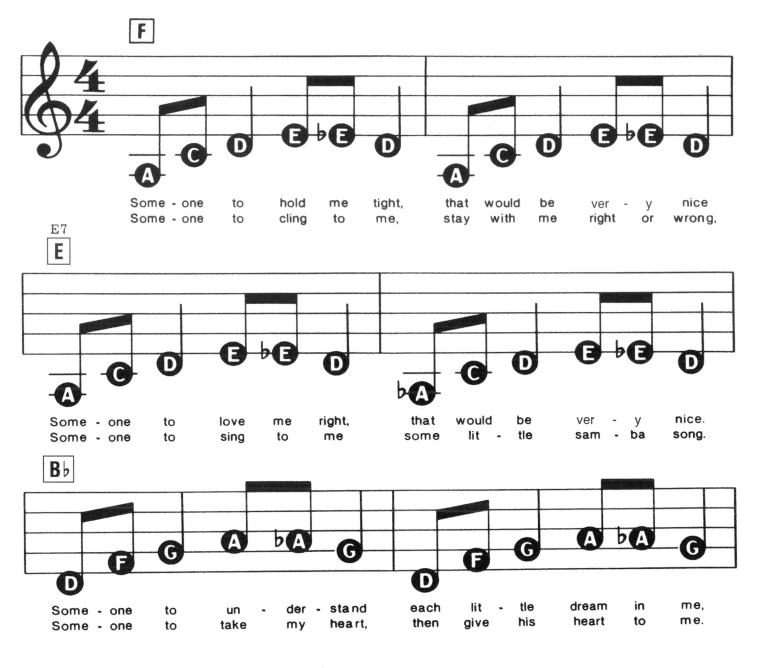

Some-one to hold me tight, that would be ver-y nice
Some-one to cling to me, stay with me right or wrong,

Some-one to love me right, that would be ver-y nice.
Some-one to sing to me some lit-tle sam-ba song.

Some-one to un-der-stand each lit-tle dream in me,
Some-one to take my heart, then give his heart to me.

some-one to take my hand, to be a team with me.
Some-one who's read-y to give love a start with me.

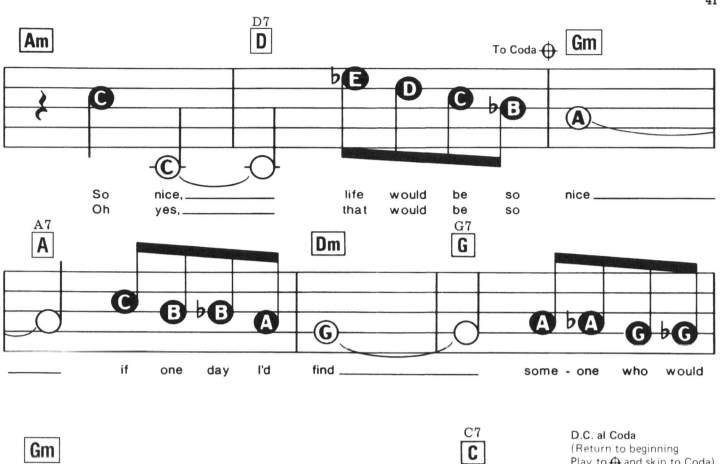

So nice,_____ life would be so nice _____
Oh yes,_____ that would be so

_____ if one day I'd find _____ some-one who would

take my hand and sam-ba thru life with me.

⊕ CODA

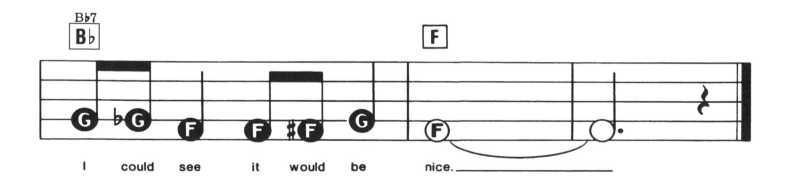

nice._____ Should it be you and me

I could see it would be nice._____

Tango of Roses

Registration 4
Rhythm: Tango

Words by Marjorie Harper
Music by Vittorio Mascheroni

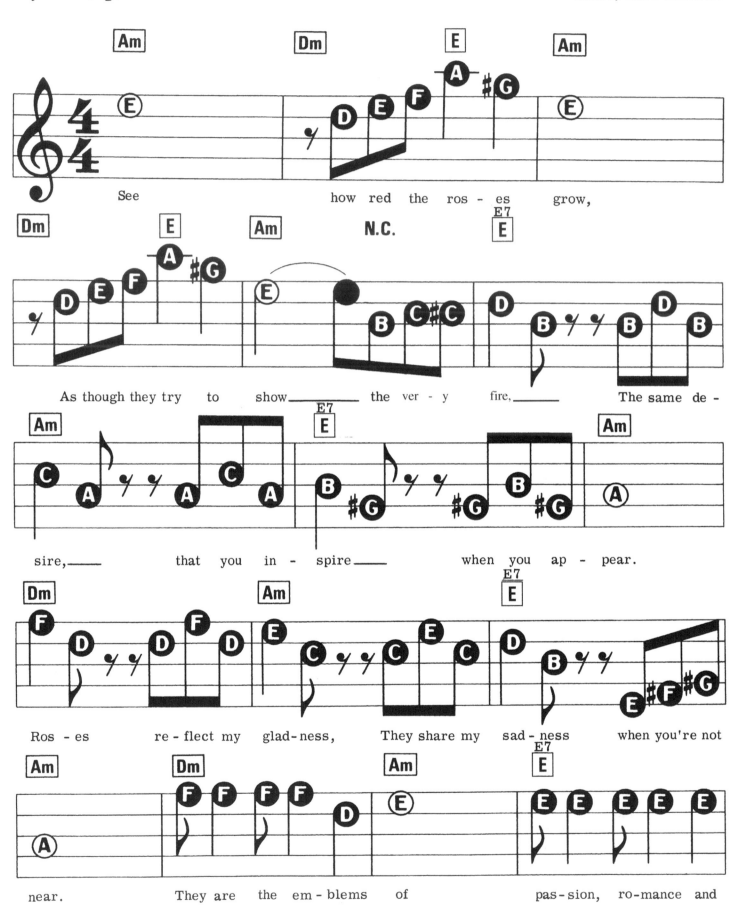

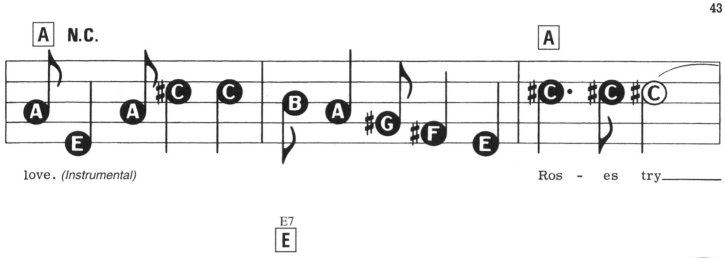

love. *(Instrumental)*   Ros - es try____

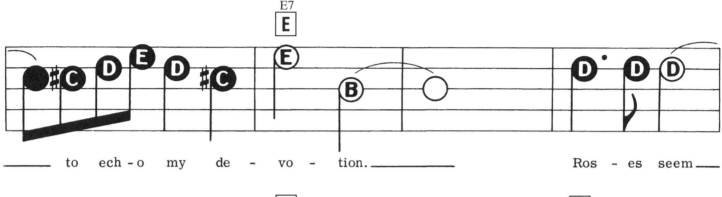

____ to ech -o my de - vo - tion.____   Ros - es seem____

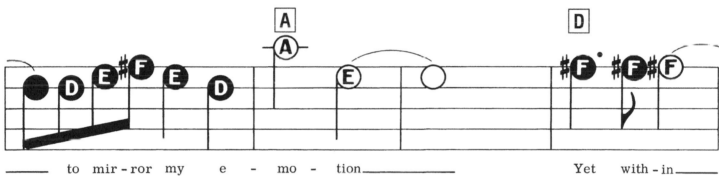

____ to mir - ror my e - mo - tion____   Yet with - in____

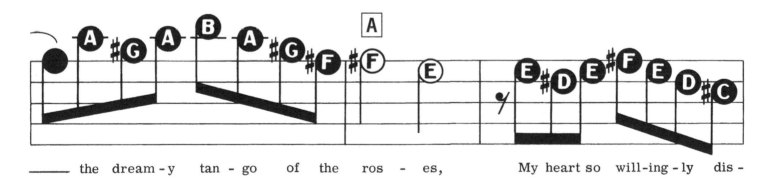

____ the dream -y tan - go of the ros - es,   My heart so will-ing-ly dis -

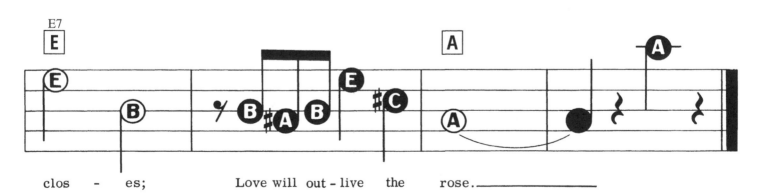

clos - es;   Love will out - live the rose.____

Tristeza
(Goodbye Sadness)

Registration 4
Rhythm: Bossa Nova or Latin

Music by Harold Lobo
Portuguese Words by Niltinho
English Words by Norman Gimbel

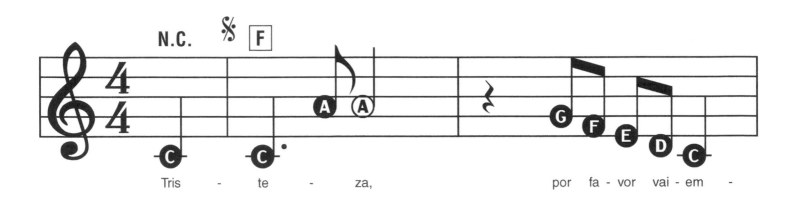

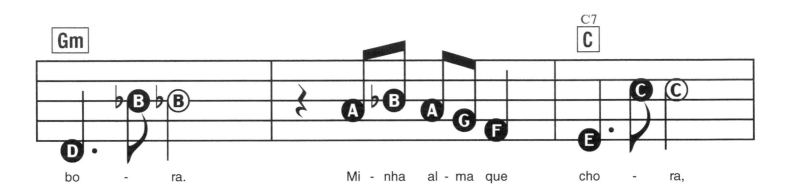

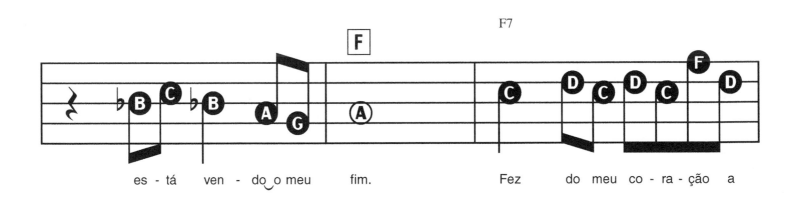

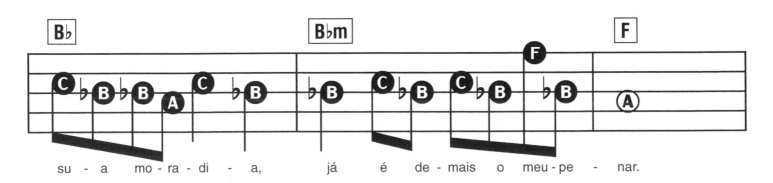

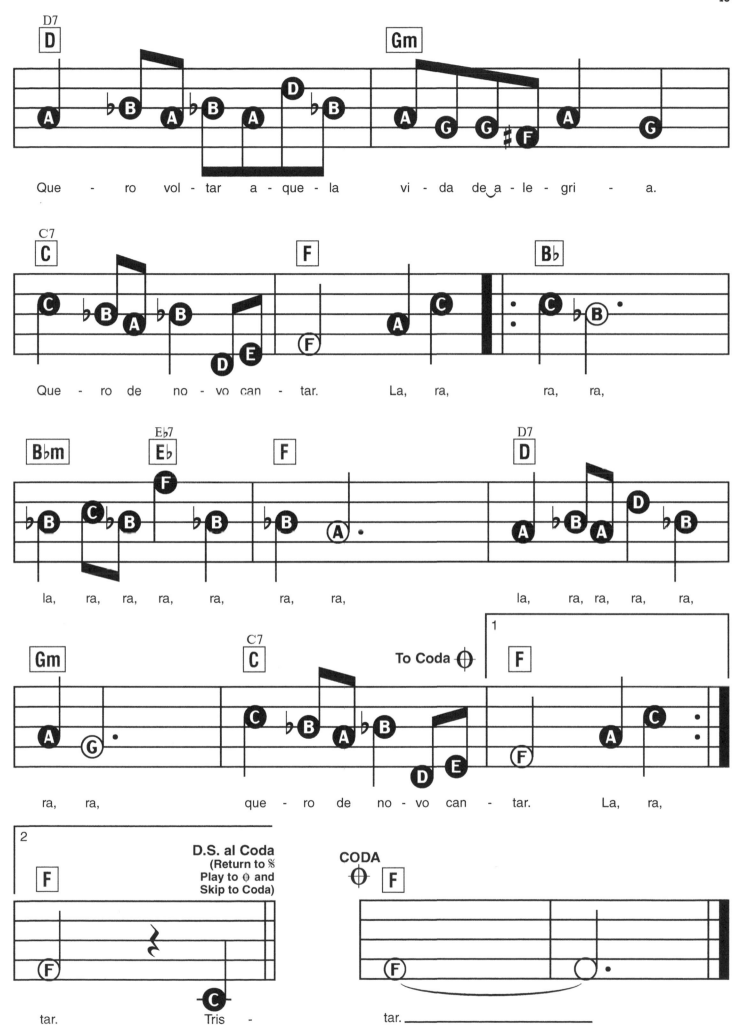

Telephone Song

Registration 2
Rhythm: Bossa Nova or Latin

English Words by Norman Gimbel
Portuguese Words by Ronaldo Boscoli
Music by Roberto Menescal

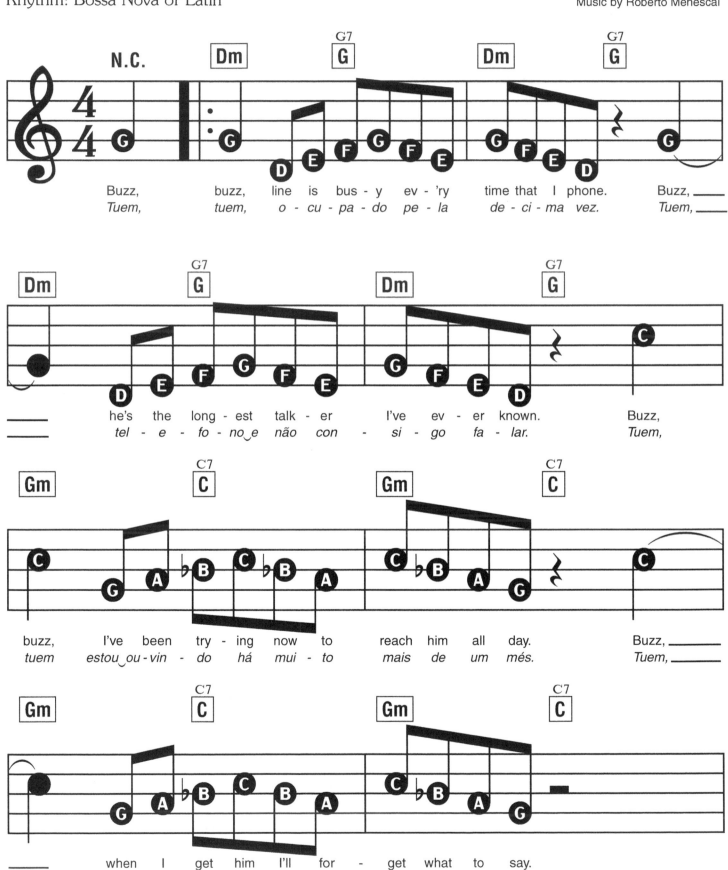

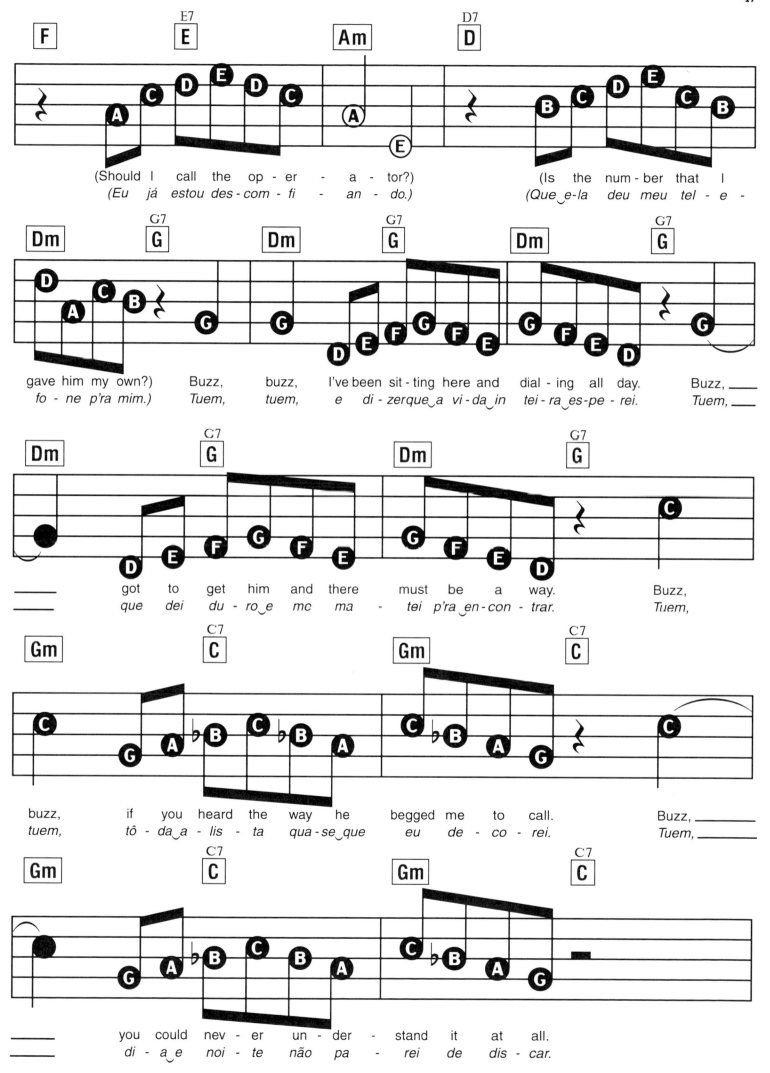

48

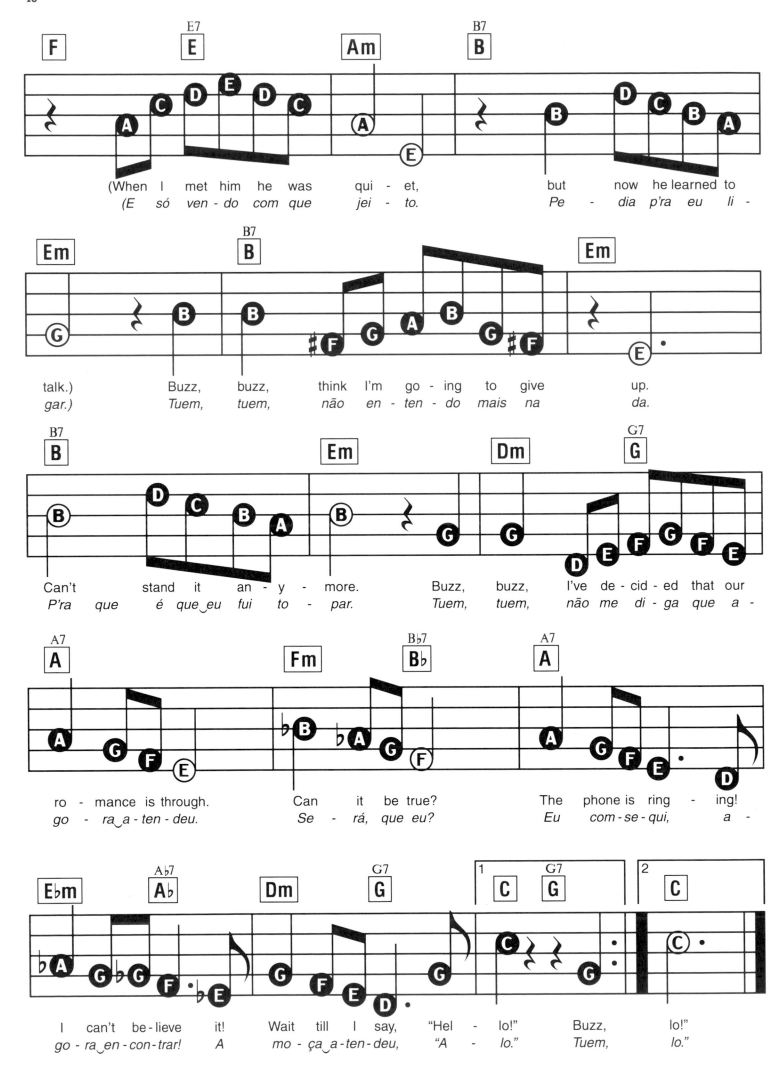